John Rutter
CAROLS

JOY TO THE WORLD!

Fifteen sacred carols and Christmas hymns for mixed voices

EDITED AND ARRANGED
BY JOHN RUTTER

MUSIC DEPARTMENT

OXFORD
UNIVERSITY PRESS

PREFACE

JOY TO THE WORLD! presents fifteen of the finest and best-loved sacred carols and Christmas hymns in choral arrangements which may be performed either separately, or else as a sequence (with or without readings and prayers) forming a complete Christmas service or concert.

Each arrangement is complete in itself, so the suggested sequence (shown with readings and prayers on p. 58) can be shortened or altered to suit the needs of different choirs and occasions.

Five Christmas hymns are included, in arrangements for choir, congregation/audience, and organ or orchestra. The opening hymn, *O come all ye faithful,* is preceded by an optional fanfare for brass, percussion, and organ. In addition, *Joy To The World* is presented in a special extended arrangement for choir. Six carols are arranged for unaccompanied choir, and three for choir with piano, organ, or orchestra.

Instrumentation for the accompanied items is listed at the foot of their first pages. The hymns are scored for full orchestra, but any of the woodwind, brass and percussion may be omitted if organ is available. The carols are scored for small orchestra, or less. All the accompaniments may satisfactorily be played by piano or organ alone.

Companion volumes of the John Rutter Carols:

O HOLY NIGHT (thirteen sacred carols and Christmas hymns)
WE WISH YOU A MERRY CHRISTMAS (twelve secular carols and Christmas songs)

Note:
Orchestral scores and parts are available from Oxford University Press.

CONTENTS

Carols suitable for unaccompanied singing are marked thus: *

TITLE PAGE

O come, all ye faithful 1
J.F. Wade arr. John Rutter

*Lo, how a rose e'er blooming 7
Old German arr. M. Praetorius

*'Twas in the moon of winter time 8
Canadian trad. arr. John Rutter

Joy to the world! 13
Lowell Mason arr. John Rutter

It came upon the midnight clear 20
R.S. Willis arr. John Rutter

*Away in a manger 22
W.J. Kirkpatrick arr. John Rutter

*Silent night 24
Franz Grüber arr. John Rutter

O little town of Bethlehem 28
Lewis Redner arr. John Rutter

*Rise up, shepherd, and follow 30
Spiritual arr. John Rutter

*In dulci jubilo 33
German 14th -cent. arr. B. Gesius

How great our joy! 34
German trad. arr. John Rutter

While shepherds watched their flocks 38
Handel arr. John Rutter

Three kings of Orient 40
J.H. Hopkins arr. John Rutter

Bring a torch, Jeannette, Isabella 47
(Un flambeau, Jeannette, Isabelle)
French trad. arr. John Rutter

God rest you merry, gentlemen 54
English trad. arr. John Rutter

A service of readings and carols 58

O COME, ALL YE FAITHFUL

(Adeste fideles)

for Mixed Voices, S. A. T. B., Opt. Choir or Congregation with Organ*

Words tr.
F. OAKELEY, W. T. BROOKE
and others

J. F. WADE (?)
arranged by JOHN RUTTER
(verses 6 and 7)

Soprano
Alto
(Organ)
Tenor
Bass

1. O come, all ye faith - ful, Joy - ful and tri - um - phant, O come_ ye, O come__ ye to Beth - le - hem; Come and be - hold_ him Born the King of An - gels: *O come, let us a - dore him, O come, let us a - dore him, O come, let us a - dore__ him, _ Christ __ the Lord!*

2. God of ___ God, ___ Light_ of ___ Light, ___ Lo! __ he ab - hors__ not the Vir - gin's womb; Ve - ry __ God, _ Be - -got -ten, not cre - a - ted:

Man.

Ped.

3. See how the shepherds,
Summoned to his cradle,
Leaving their flocks, draw nigh with lowly fear;
We too will thither
Bend our joyful footsteps:
O come, etc.

4. Lo! star - led chieftains,
Magi, Christ adoring,
Offer him incense, gold, and myrrh;
We to the Christ Child
Bring our hearts' oblations:
O come, etc.

5. Child, for us sinners
Poor and in the manger,
Fain we embrace thee, with awe and love;
Who would not love thee,
Loving us so dearly?
O come, etc.

To next page for verse 6

Instrumentation: 2Fl, 2Ob, 2Cl, Bsn, 2Hn, 3Tpt, 2Tbn, B. Tbn, Tba, Timp, Perc, Organ, Strings. Woodwind, brass and percussion are optional if organ is available. This arrangement is preceded by an optional fanfare for 2Hn, 3Tpt, 2Tbn, B. Tbn, Tba, Timp, Perc, Organ (optional). Score and parts are included with the orchestral rental material for the hymn. Orchestral scores and parts are available on rental.

© Hinshaw Music, Inc. 1981. Assigned to Oxford University Press 2016 Printed in Great Britain

The Moral Rights of the Arranger have been asserted. Photocopying this copyright material is ILLEGAL

Descant (Sopranos)
f
No-well, no - well, no-well, no -well. Sing, O sing in ex-ul-ta -
Melody (all other voices)
f
6. Sing, choirs of an - gels, Sing in ex - ul - ta - tion,
Gt. + Sw.
Organ
f
Tuba
Ped.
- - tion, Sing, all ye cit - i -zens of hea - ven, of
Sing, all ye cit - i - zens of heav'n a -
cresc.
ff
hea - ven a -bove; Glo - ry, glo-ry to God,
ff
-bove; Glo - ry to God
Gt. + Sw.
ff

To the next page for verse 7

Choir 1 and Congregation
f unis.
7. Yea, Lord, we greet thee, Born this hap - py
Choir 2 (optional)
f
7. Yea, Lord, we greet thee, Born this hap - py
f
Organ
Gt.+ Sw.
f
morn - ing, Je - su, to thee be glo - ry
morn - ing, Je - su,
morn - ing, Je - su, to thee be glo - ry

Largamente (very broad)
ff
giv'n; Word of the Fa - ther,
Fa - ther,
giv'n; Word of the Fa - ther, of the Fa - ther,
Largamente (very broad)
cresc.
ff
Tuba
a tempo
mf
f
Now in flesh ap - pear - ing: O come, let us a - dore him, O
Now in flesh ap - pear - ing:
Now in flesh ap - pear - ing: O come, a - dore him,
a tempo
mf
Gt. + Sw.
f

Largamente
ff
come, let us a - dore him, O come, let us a -
f
ff
O come, a - dore him, O come, a -
f
ff
Largamente
ff
- dore him, Christ the Lord!
him, Christ the Lord!
- dore him, Christ the Lord!

LO, HOW A ROSE E'ER BLOOMING

Original German text, 16th century
Tr. THEODORE BAKER

Old German Tune
arranged by
M. PRAETORIUS (1571-1621)

Soprano
Alto

1. Lo, how a Rose e'er bloom-ing From ten-der stem _ hath
* 2. I - sai-ah 'twas fore-told it, The Rose I have _ in

ten - der stem hath
Rose - I have in

Tenor
Bass

ten-der stem hath
Rose I have in

sprung! Of Jes-se's lin-eage com-ing As men of old ___ have
mind, With Ma-ry we be-hold it, The Vir-gin Mo - ther

men ___ of old have
Vir - gin Mo - ther

men of old have
Vir-gin Mo - ther

sung. It came, a flow-'ret bright, ___ A -
kind. To show God's love a - right, ___ She

-mid the cold of win - ter, When half spent ___ was ___ the night.
bore to men a Sa - vior, When half spent ___ was ___ the night.

was the night.

* Soprano and Tenor may exchange parts in verse 2 to good effect. Verse 1 may be repeated after verse 2.

'TWAS IN THE MOON OF WINTER TIME

for Mixed Voices, S. A. T. B., *a cappella*

Words by
JEAN DE BRÉBEUF (1593-1649)
Tr. J. E. Middleton

Canadian traditional tune
arranged by
JOHN RUTTER

Andante con moto

Soprano

Alto

Tenor

Bass

mp *mf* *p* *Hum*

p cresc. *mf* *p* *Hum*

p *cresc.* *mp* *mp* *Hum* 1. 'Twas

div. p *cresc.* *mf* *p* *Hum*

in the moon of win - ter time, When all the birds had fled, That

© Oxford University Press 1981. Photocopying this copyright material is ILLEGAL

migh - ty Git - chi Man - i - tou Sent an - gel choirs in - stead; Be -
-fore their light the stars grew dim, And won -d'ring hun -ters heard the hymn:
unis.
mp
cresc.
Je - sus your King is born, Je - sus is born, In ex-cel - sis
mp
cresc.
(Hum)
mp
cresc.
Je - sus your King is born, Je - sus is born, In ex-cel - sis
mp
cresc.
(Hum)

f
glo - ri - a.
p legato
div.
2. With - in a lodge of
f
p legato
2. With - in a
f
glo - ri - a.
f
div.
unis.
bro - ken bark The ten - der babe was found, A rag - ged robe of
lodge The ten - der babe was found, A rag - ged robe
p legato
A robe of
mp
rab - bit skin En - wrapped his beau - ty round; Ah
mp
of skin Wrapped his beau - ty round; Ah
mf
skin Wrapped his beau - ty round; But as the hun - ter
mf
But as the hun - ter

f
Je - sus your
f
Ah
Je - sus your
f
braves drew nigh, The an - gel song rang loud and high:
Je - sus your
braves drew nigh, The an - gel song rang loud and high:
King is born.
Ah
Ah
King is born.
Ah
King is born, Je - sus is born, In ex-cel - sis glo - ri -
f
Je - sus is born, In ex-cel - sis glo - ri -
mf
f
S.
A.
3. O chil - dren of the fo - rest free, O
-a.
T.
B.
mf
f

sons of Man - i - tou, The ho - ly child of earth and heav'n is

S. Come, kneel be - fore the ra - diant boy, Who
mf
A.
born to - day for you.
T. Ah
B.
mf

brings you beau - ty, peace, and joy:
f
Je - sus your King is born,
f Je - sus your

Largamente
ff
Je - sus is born, In ex - cel - sis glo - ri - a.
ff

JOY TO THE WORLD!

(extended arrangement)

for Mixed Voices, S. A. T. B., with Keyboard*

Words by
ISAAC WATTS

Melody by LOWELL MASON (1792-1872)
(based on HANDEL)
arranged by JOHN RUTTER

* Instrumentation: 2Ob, Bsn, 2Tpt, Timp, Organ or Harpsichord, Strings. Orchestral scores and parts are available on rental.
A simple harmonization of this hymn, suitable for unaccompanied or congegational use, is included in the companion volume, O HOLY NIGHT.

© Hinshaw Music, Inc. 1981. Assigned to Oxford University Press 2016. Photocopying this copyright material is ILLEGAL

ev - 'ry heart pre - pare him room, And
glo - ries of his right - eous - ness, And
heav'n and na - ture sing, And heav'n and na - ture sing, And
won-ders of his love, And won-ders of his love, And
And heav'n and na - ture sing, And heav'n and na - ture
And won-ders of his love, And won-ders of his
after v.4: to CODA (p.19)
heav'n, and heav'n and na - ture sing.
won - ders, won - ders of his love.
sing, and heav'n and na - ture sing.
love, and won -ders of his love.
after v.4: to CODA (p.19)

tr
mf
A
mf
2. Joy to the earth! the Sa - vior reigns:
mf
Let
mf
A
men their songs em - ploy;
While

Rocks, hills and plains Re -
fields and floods,
Re -
Re -
f
-peat the sound-ing joy, Re - peat the sound-ing joy, Re -
-peat the sound-ing joy, Re - peat the sound-ing joy, Re -
f
f
-peat the sound-ing joy, the sound-ing joy.
-peat, re- peat the sound-ing joy.
-peat, re - peat the sound-ing joy.
mf

tr
f
p
B
S.
A.
mf
3. No more let sins and sor - rows grow, sor - rows
T.
B.
mf
3. No more let sins and sor - rows
B
tr
tr
mf
3. No more let sins and sor - rows grow,
grow, and sor - rows grow, Nor
grow, let sins and sor - rows, sor - rows grow,

p
He
thorns in - fest the ground;
mf
dim.
thorns in - fest the
mf
dim.
thorns in - fest the
(p)
cresc.
comes to make his bless - ings flow Far as the curse is found, Far,
p
cresc.
Far as the curse is found, Far,
p
cresc.
ground, he comes to make his bless - ings flow, his bless- ings flow, Far,
p
cresc.
ground, Far,
f

f
far as the curse is found.
f
far as the curse is found.
f
far as the curse is found.
f
far as the curse is found.
D. S. for Verse 4
(back to p. 13)
Coda (from p. 14)
D. S. for Verse 4
(back to p. 13)
Coda (from p. 14)
tr

IT CAME UPON THE MIDNIGHT CLEAR

Words by
E. H. SEARS

R. S. WILLIS (1819-1900)
Descant by JOHN RUTTER

Soprano Descant (Verse 4)
(All other voices sing melody)

4. For lo! the days are hast - 'ning on, By

Soprano
Alto

1. It came up - on the mid - night clear, That
2. Still through the clo - ven skies they come, With
3. Yet with the woes of sin and strife The
4. For lo! the days are hast - 'ning on, By

Tenor
Bass

pro - phet - bards fore - told, When with, with the ev - er -

glo - rious song of old, From an - gels bend - ing
peace - ful wings un - furled; And still their hea - v'nly
world has suf - fered long; Be - neath the an - gel -
pro - phet - bards fore - told, When, with the ev - er -

cir - cling years, Comes round the age of

near the earth To touch their harps of
mu - sic floats O'er all the wea - ry
strain have rolled Two thou - sand years of
cir - cling years, Comes round the age of

Instrumentation: 2Fl, 2Ob, 2Cl, Bsn, 2Hn, 2Tpt, 2Tbn, B. Tbn, Tba, Timp, Strings. Woodwind, brass and percussion are optional if organ is available. Orchestral scores and parts are available on rental.

© Hinshaw Music, Inc. 1981. Assigned to Oxford University Press 2016. Photocopying this copyright material is ILLEGAL

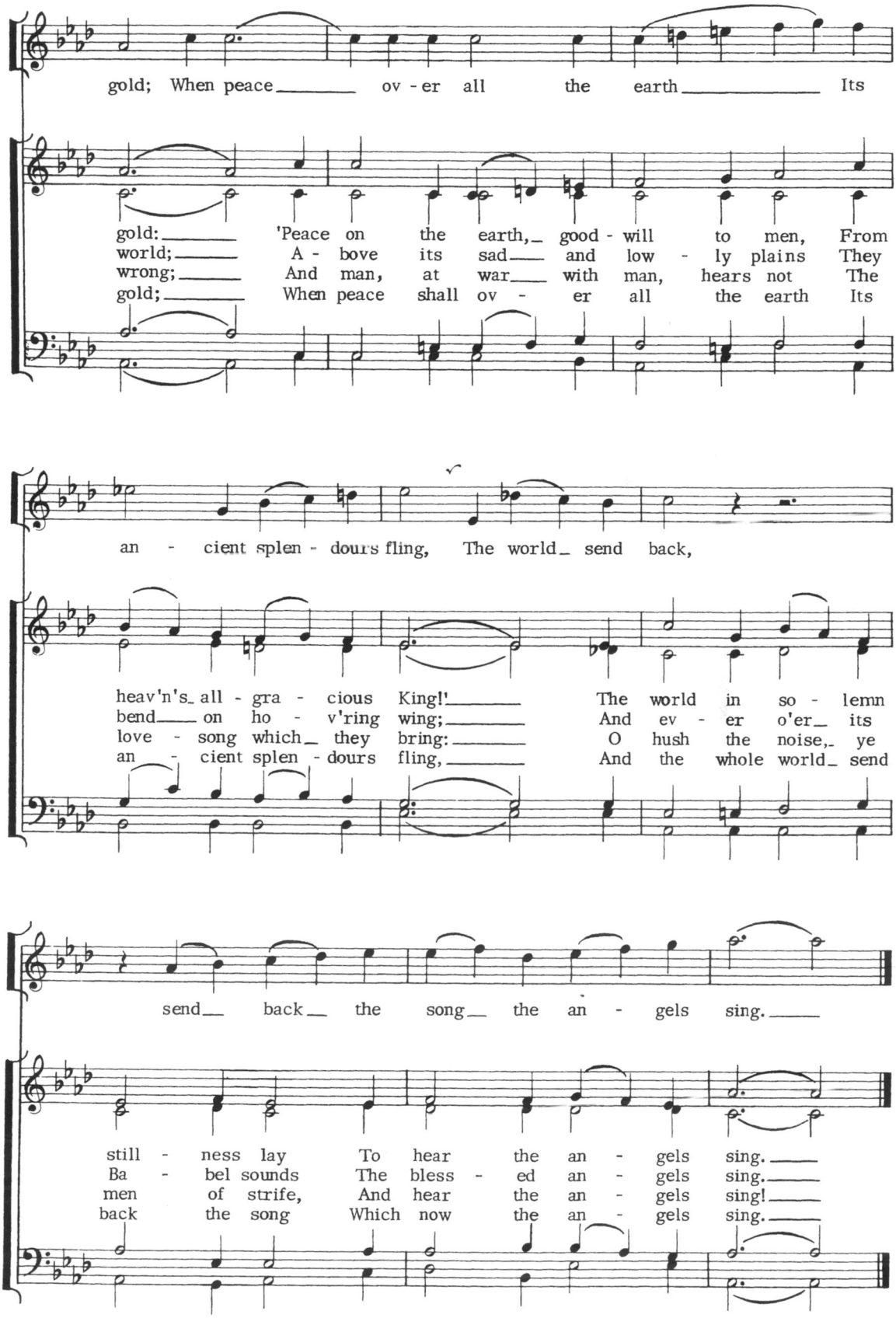
gold; When peace ov - er all the earth Its
gold: 'Peace on the earth, good - will to men, From
world; A - bove its sad and low - ly plains They
wrong; And man, at war with man, hears not The
gold; When peace shall ov - er all the earth Its
an - cient splen - dours fling, The world send back,
heav'n's all - gra - cious King! The world in so - lemn
bend on ho - v'ring wing; And ev - er o'er its
love - song which they bring: O hush the noise, ye
an - cient splen - dours fling, And the whole world send
send back the song the an - gels sing.
still - ness lay To hear the an - gels sing.
Ba - bel sounds The bless - ed an - gels sing.
men of strife, And hear the an - gels sing!
back the song Which now the an - gels sing.

AWAY IN A MANGER

*(Original tune)**

for Mixed Voices, S. A. T. B., a cappella

Words anon.

Melody by
W. J. KIRKPATRICK (1838-1921)
arranged by JOHN RUTTER

*An accompanied arrangement of the setting of this text by J. R. Murray is included in the companion volume, O HOLY NIGHT.

© Oxford University Press 1981. Photocopying this copyright material is ILLEGAL

p
Hum
mp unis.
2. The cat - tle are low - ing, the ba - by a - wakes, But
lit - tle Lord Je - sus no cry - ing he makes. I
love thee, Lord Je - sus! Look down from the sky, And
D. C. for verse 3
stay by my side un - til morn - ing is nigh.

SILENT NIGHT

for Mixed Voices, S. A. T. B., *a cappella*

German Words by
JOSEF MOHR
Tr. J. F. YOUNG

FRANZ GRÜBER
arranged by
JOHN RUTTER

Andante espressivo

Soprano

Alto

Tenor

Bass

p

1. Si - lent night!

p

1. Si - lent night!

p legato

div.

pp

Hum

p legato

div.

pp

Hum

ho - ly night! All is calm, all is bright Round yon vir - gin

ho - ly night! All is calm, all is bright Round yon vir - gin

© Oxford University Press 1981. Photocopying this copyright material is ILLEGAL

cresc.
mo - ther and child. Ho - ly in - fant so ten - der and mild,
cresc.
mo - ther and child. Ho - ly in - fant so ten - der and mild,
cresc.
cresc.
mp
p
Sleep in hea - ven-ly peace, Sleep in hea - ven-ly peace.
mp
p
Sleep in hea - ven-ly peace, Sleep in hea - ven-ly peace.
p
pp
p
pp
div. p
Aw Aw
p
Aw Aw
mf dolce cantabile
unis.
2. Si - lent night! ho - ly night! Shep-herds quake
p
Aw Aw

mp
Al-le - lu - ia, al - le - lu - ia, al-le- lu - ia, al - le -
mp
Al-le - lu- ia, al - le - lu - ia, al- le - lu - ia, al - le -
f
at the sight. Glo-ries stream from hea - ven a-far, Heav'n-ly hosts sing
mp
Aw Aw
cresc.
f
poco rit.
mf
- lu - ia, Christ the Sa-vior is born, al-le - lu-ia, al-le-lu - ia,
cresc.
f
mf
- lu - ia, Christ the Sa-vior is born, al-le - lu-ia, al-le-lu - ia,
cresc.
ff
f
al - le-lu-ia; Christ, the Sa - vior is born! Christ, the Sa - vior is
cresc.
unis. f
mf
Christ the Sa - vior is born! Al - le-lu - ia,
a tempo
p
p
al - le- lu-ia. 3. Si - lent night! ho - ly night!
p
p
al - le - lu -ia. 3. Si - lent night! ho - ly night!
p
div.
unis.
born! Al-le-lu-ia. 3. Si - lent night! ho - ly night!
p
Ah, ah, ah 3. Si-lent night! ho - ly

cresc.
mf
Son of God, love's pure light Ra - diant beams from thy
Son of God, love's pure light Ra-diant beams from thy
Son of God, love's pure light Ra-diant beams from thy
night! Son of God, Ra - diant beams from thy
div.
f
ho - ly face, With the dawn of re - deem-ing grace, Je - sus, Lord, at thy
ho - ly face, With the dawn of re - deem-ing grace, Je-sus, Lord
ho - ly face, With the dawn of re - deem-ing grace, Je-sus, Lord, at thy
unis.
ho - ly face, With the dawn of re - deem - ing grace, Je-sus Lord, at thy
ritard.
a tempo
rit.
mp dim.
p
dim.
pp
ppp
birth, Je - sus, Lord, at thy birth.
at thy birth, Je-sus, Lord, at thy birth. Hum
birth, Je - sus, Lord.
Hum
birth, Je - sus, Lord.
Hum

O LITTLE TOWN OF BETHLEHEM

Words by
PHILLIPS BROOKS

LEWIS REDNER (1831-1908)
Descant by JOHN RUTTER

Soprano Descant (Verse 4)
(All other voices sing melody)

4. O ho - ly child of Beth - le - hem, Des - cend to_ us, des-

Soprano
Alto

1. O lit - tle town of Beth - le - hem, How still we_ see thee
2. O morn-ing stars, to - ge - ther Pro - claim the_ ho - ly
3. How si - lent - ly, how si - lent - ly The won - drous gift is
4. O ho - ly child of Beth - le - hem, Des - cend to_ us, we

Tenor
Bass

-cend to us; Cast out our sin, Be

lie! A - bove thy deep and dream - less sleep The
birth, And prai - ses sing to God the King, And
giv'n! So God im - parts to hu - man hearts The
pray; Cast out our sin, and en - ter in, Be

Original key G. Alto and tenor parts in the penultimate measure adapted.

Instrumentation: 2Fl, 2Ob, 2Cl, Bsn, 2Hn, 2Tpt, 2Tbn, B. Tbn, Tba, Timp, Strings. Woodwind, brass and timp are optional if organ is available. Orchestral scores and parts are available on rental.

© Hinshaw Music, Inc. 1981. Assigned to Oxford University Press 2016. Photocopying this copyright material is ILLEGAL

born in us to - day. We hear the Christ - mas
si - lent stars go by. Yet in thy dark streets
peace to men on earth; For Christ is born of
bless - ings of his heav'n. No ear may hear his
born in us to - day. We hear the Christ - mas
an - gels The great glad ti - dings tell: O come,
shi - neth The ev - er - last - ing light; The
Ma - ry; And, gath - ered all a - bove, While
com - ing; But in this world of sin, Where
an - gels The great glad ti - dings tell: O
O come, O come, Our Lord Em-ma-nu - el.
hopes and fears of all the years Are met in thee to - night.
mor - tals sleep, the an - gels keep Their watch of won - d'ring love.
meek souls will re - ceive him, still The dear Christ en - ters in.
come to us, a - bide with us, Our Lord Em - ma - nu - el.

RISE UP, SHEPHERD, AND FOLLOW

for Mixed Voices, S. A. T. B., *a cappella*

Spiritual
arranged by
JOHN RUTTER

Andante animato (♩ = 66)

ritard.

Soprano: *f* *mf* *mp* *legato*
Fol-low, fol- low, fol -low the -

Alto: *f* *mf* *mp* *legato*
Fol-low, fol - low, fol -low the

Tenor: *f* *mf* *mp* *legato*
Rise up, rise up, fol - low the

Bass: *f* *mf* *mp*
Rise up, rise up,

Più mosso

Tenor Solo *mf*
1. There's a star in the east on Christ-mas morn,
2. take good heed to the an -gel's word,

S. A. *p* (*p*)
star.
1. *Hum*
2. *Aw*

T. B. *p* (*p*)
Ah

optional
Rise up, shep-herd, and fol - low, It will lead to the place where the
You'll for - get your flock, you'll for -

(T.B.) *Rise up, shep-herd, and fol - low,*
1. *Hum*
2. *Aw*
mp

© Oxford University Press 1981. Photocopying this copyright material is ILLEGAL

3
Sa -vior's born;
- get your herd;
Rise up, shep-herd, and fol - low.
(T.) Rise up, shep-herd, and fol - low.
f
Leave your flocks and leave your lambs, Rise up, shep-herd, and fol -low;
mp
mp 1. Hum
mf 2. Rise up, shep-herd, and fol -low;
(1. and 2.) fol-low
mp
Leave your sheep and leave your rams, Rise up, shep-herd, and fol- low.
(2.) fol - low.
mp Hum
mp Aw
mp Hum
mf Rise up, shep-herd, and fol - low.
f legato
mf
Fol - low, fol - low, Rise up, shep-herd, and fol- low;
f legato
fol -low;
mf

mf
p
3
Fol - low the star of Beth - le - hem, Rise up, shep-herd, and
mf
p
Rise up, and
1st time
2nd time
Meno mosso
pp
p
fol - low.
fol - low.
Fol - low,
fol - low.
fol - low.
Fol - low,
Solo
mf
pp
fol - low. 2. If you fol - low.
pp
mp
fol - low.
fol - low.
Hum
rit.
pp
fol - low, fol - low the star.
pp
fol - low, fol - low the star.
p
pp
Hum fol - low the star.
p
p
pp
Hum

IN DULCI JUBILO

Original text 14th century
*Tr. R. L. PEARSALL**

German, 14th century
Arranged by
B. GESIUS (1601)

(Con moto)

Soprano
Alto

1. In dul - ci ju - bi - lo Let us our hom - age shew; Our heart's joy re - cli - neth In prae - se - pi - o And like a bright star shi - neth Ma - tris in gre - mi - o. Al - pha es et O, Al - pha es et O.
2. O Je - su par - vu - le! I yearn for thee al - way! Hear me, I be - seech thee, O Puer op - ti - me! My pray - er let it reach thee, O Prin - ceps glo - ri - ae! Tra - he me post te! Tra - he me post te!
3. O Pa - tris ca - ri - tas, O Na - ti le - ni - tas! Deep - ly were we stain - èd Per nos - tra cri - mi - na; But thou hast for us gain - èd Coe - lo - rum gau - di - a. O that we were there! O that we were there!
4. U - bi sunt gau - di - a, If that they be not there? There are an - gels sing - ing No - va can - ti - ca, And there the bells are ring - ing In Re - gis cu - ri - a: O that we were there! O that we were there!

Tenor
Bass

* The text given here is a translation of the one originally written for the melody. An accompanied arrangement of the same melody to the text *Good Christian men, rejoice* is included in the companion volume, O HOLY NIGHT.

HOW GREAT OUR JOY!

for Mixed Voices, S. A. T. B., with Organ*

German traditional carol
arranged by JOHN RUTTER

Brightly (♩ = c.112)
Ch. 8', 2'

Organ

mf non legato

Sw.

Ped.

V. 1: Tenors and Basses
V. 2: Sopranos and Altos

mf

1. While by the sheep we watched at night, Glad ti-dings brought an
2. There shall be born, so he did say, In Beth-le-hem a

V. 1: S. and A.
V. 2: T. and B.

f *mp*

an-gel bright.
child to-day. *How great our joy!* *Great our joy!*

V. 1: T. and B.
V. 2: S. and A.

V. 1: S. and A.
V. 2: T. and B.

V. 1: T. and B.
V. 2: S. and A.

f *mp* *f*

Joy, joy, joy! *Joy, joy, joy!* *Praise we the Lord in heav'n on high!*

* Instrumentation: 2Fl/Picc, 2Ob, 2Cl, Bsn, 2Hn, Perc, Strings.
Orchestral scores and parts are available on rental.

© Oxford University Press 1981. Photocopying this copyright material is ILLEGAL

* If preferred, Choir 1 part may be sung by a solo voice and Choir 2 part by the full choir.

(mf)
Joy, joy, joy!
Praise we the Lord in
(mp)
Joy, joy, Joy, joy, joy!
Ah
(mp)
heav'n on high!
p
Praise we the Lord in heav'n on high!
p
f
Choirs 1 and 2
4. This gift of God we'll che-rish well,
f
Gt. 8', 2'
f
Sw.
Ped.
sim.

That ev-er joy our hearts shall fill. How great our joy!
Great our joy!
(f)
Joy, joy, joy!
Joy, joy, joy!
Praise we the Lord in
p legato
mf
p legato
mf
Largamente
ff marcato
heav'n on high!
Praise we the Lord in heav'n on high!
ff marcato
Largamente
f

WHILE SHEPHERDS WATCHED THEIR FLOCKS

for Mixed Voices, S. A. T. B., with Organ*

Words by NAHUM TATE

G. F. HANDEL
Verse 6 arranged by
JOHN RUTTER

Soprano
Alto

1. While shep - herds watched their flocks by night, All
2. 'Fear not,' said he (for migh - ty dread Had

Tenor
Bass

seat - ed on the ground, The an - gel of the Lord came down, And
seized their trou - bled mind); Glad ti - dings of great joy I bring To

glo - ry shone a - round, and glo - ry shone a - round.
you and all man - kind, to you and all man - kind.

3. 'To you in David's town this day
Is born of David's line
A Saviour, who is Christ the Lord;
And this shall be the sign:

4. 'The heavenly Babe you there shall find
To human view displayed,
All meanly wrapped in swathing bands,
And in a manger laid.'

5. Thus spake the Seraph; and forthwith
Appeared a shining throng
Of angels praising God, who thus
Addressed their joyful song:

* Instrumentation: 2Fl, 2Ob, 2Cl, Bsn, 2Hn, 2Tpt, 2Tbn, B. Tbn, Tba, Timp, Strings. Woodwind, brass and timp are optional if organ is available. Orchestral scores and parts are available on rental.

© Hinshaw Music, Inc. 1981. Assigned to Oxford University Press 2016. Photocopying this copyright material is ILLEGAL

Descant (Sopranos)
6. 'All glo - ry be to God on high, And on the earth be
All Other Voices
6. 'All glo - ry be to God on high, And on the earth be
Organ
peace; Good - will from heav'n to men
peace; Good - will hence - forth from heav'n to men Be -
Tuba
Be - gin and nev - er cease, be - gin and nev-er cease.'
-gin and nev - er cease, be - gin and nev - er cease.'

THREE KINGS OF ORIENT

(accompanied version)

for Mixed Voices, S. A. T. B., with Keyboard*

Words and Music by
J. H. HOPKINS
arranged by JOHN RUTTER

*Instrumentation: 2Fl, 2Ob, 2Cl, 2Bsn, 2Hn, Perc, Hp, Strings. Orchestral scores and parts are available on rental.
An unaccompanied arrangement of this carol is included in the companion volume, O HOLY NIGHT.

© Oxford University Press 1981. Photocopying this copyright material is ILLEGAL

(Hum)
foun - tain, Moor and moun - tain, Fol-low-ing yon - der star:
Cl.
A Refrain for Verses 1, 2 and 3
p
O star of won - der, star of night, Star with roy - al
p
A
(p)
Fl.
mp cresc.
mf
beau - ty bright; West - ward lead - ing, Still pro - ceed - ing,
mp cresc.
mf
Ob.

mp
B Verses 2 and 3
Guide us to thy per - fect light.
mp
B Verses 2 and 3
p
p
V. 2: Tenor Solo or Semi-Chorus
V. 3: Baritone Solo or Semi-Chorus
mf
2. Born a king on Beth-le-hem plain, Gold I bring to crown him a-gain,
3. Frank-in - cense to of-fer have I, In-cense owns a De - i-ty nigh,
Pno.
S.
A.
p 2. Hum
mp 3. Aw
T.
B.
Pno.
cresc.
f
dim.
Refrain D. S.
(back to p. 41)
King for ev - er, Ceas-ing nev - er, O - ver us all to reign:
Prayer and prais - ing, All men rais - ing, Wor-ship him, God most high:
cresc.
dim.
cresc.
dim.

C Verse 4
Bass Solo or Semi-Chorus
mp
4. Myrrh is mine; its bit - ter per - fume
Bsn.
p
Breathes a life of ga - ther - ing gloom; Sor - row - ing,
Str.
ritard.
a tempo
sigh - ing, Bleed - ing, dy - ing, Sealed in the stone - cold tomb:
T.
mp
O star of won - der, star of night, Star with
B.
div.
mp
(Accomp. tacet)

roy - al beau - ty bright; West - ward lead - ing,
Still pro - ceed - ing, Guide us to thy per - fect light.
D
S.
A.
f sonore
5. Glo - rious now be -
T.
B.
f sonore
D
Str.
f

-hold him a - rise, King, and God, and sa - cri -
cresc.
div.
ff
-fice! Heav'n sings Al - le - lu - ia: Al - le -
cresc.
ff
cresc.
ff
mf rit.
E
a tempo
-lu - ia earth re - plies: O star of
-lu - ia the
mf
Fl.
E
mf rit.
a tempo

won - der, star of night, Star with roy - al
Star with
beau - ty bright; West - ward lead - ing, Still pro - ceed - ing,
dim.
p
rall. al fine
dim.
pp
Guide us to thy per - fect light.
p
dim.
pp
rall. al fine
Fl.
p
pp
Tamb.

BRING A TORCH, JEANNETTE, ISABELLA

(Un flambeau, Jeannette, Isabelle)

for Mixed Voices, S. A. T. B., with Piano*

English tr. by
E. C. NUNN

French traditional carol
arranged by JOHN RUTTER

Quite relaxed; a gentle one-in-the-bar (♩. = 60)

Piano

Obs.

mf

Bsns.

Drum

etc.

Sopranos and Altos

unis. mf

S.
A.

1. Bring a torch, Jean-
1. Un flam - beau, Jean-

T.
B.

Fls.

Obs.

-nette, Is - a - bel - la! Bring a torch, to the cra - dle run!
-nette, Is - a - bel - le, Un flam - beau, cou - rons au ber - ceau!

* Instrumentation: 2Fl, 2Ob, 2Bsn, Perc, Strings (optional). Orchestral scores and parts are available.

© Oxford University Press 1981. Photocopying this copyright material is ILLEGAL

A div.
It is Je - sus, good folk of the vil - lage, Christ is born and
C'est Jé - sus, bon-nes gens du ha - meau, Le Christ est né, Ma -
mf
It is Je - sus, good folk,
C'est Jé - sus, bon-nes gens,
A
mp
Ma - ry's call - ing, Ah! ah! beau - ti - ful is the
-rie ap - pel - le, Ah! ah! que la mère est
ah!
mp
mp
Ah!
Ah!
How fair the
la mère est
Fls.
mp

B
(mp)
Moth - er! Ah! ah! beau-ti - ful is her Son.
bel - le, Ah! ah! que l'En - fant est beau!
mf
Moth - er! Ah! ah! beau-ti - ful is her Son.
bel - le, Ah! ah! ah! que l'En - fant est beau!
B
p
Hum
p
p
Tacet to D
Soprano Solo or Semi-Chorus
mp dolce espress.
2. It is wrong when the Child is sleep - ing, It is wrong to
2. C'est un tort quand l'En - fant som - meil - le, C'est un tort de cri -
S.
A.
T.
B.

C
p
talk so loud. Si - lence, all, as you ga - ther a -
-er si fort. Tai - sez - vous, l'un et l'au - tre d'a -
pp
Si - lence, si -
Tai - sez - vous, tai - sez -
pp
-round, Lest your noise should wa - ken Je - sus: Hush!
-bord! Au moin-dre bruit, Jé - sus s'é - veil - le. Chut!
(pp sempre)
-lence, si - lence, hush your noise, Hush!
vous, tai - sez - vous, l'un et l'au - tre. Chut!
(pp sempre)
Hush! see how fast he slum - bers; Hush!
chut! chut! il dort à mer - veil - le, Chut!
Hush! Hush! Hush! Hush! Hush!
chut! chut! chut! chut! chut!

D
Hush! see how fast he sleeps!
chut! chut! voy -ez comme il dort!
Hush! how he sleeps!
chut! comme il dort!
Hush! Hush! Hush! he sleeps!
chut! chut! chut! il dort!
D
Obs.
p
Fls.
p
3. Soft - ly to the lit - tle sta - ble, Soft - ly for a mo - ment
3. Dou - ce - ment dans l'é - ta - ble clo - se, Dou - ce - ment, ve - nez un mo -
p

mf
come! Look and see how charm-ing is Je - sus, How he is
-ment! Ap - pro - chez, que Jé - sus est char - mant! Comme il est
mf
Look and see
Ap - pro - chez!
Fls.
mp
mf
E
p
white, His cheeks are ro - sy! Hush! Hush! See how the
blanc, comme il est ro - se! Do! Do! Do! que l'En-
p
ro - sy! Hush! Hush! how the
ro - se! Do! Do! que l'En-
E
Obs.
tr
p

rit.
Child is sleep - ing; Hush! Hush! see how he smiles in
-fant re - po - se! Do! Do! Do! qu'il rit en dor -
Child is sleep - ing; Hush! Hush! how he smiles in
-fant re - po - se! Do! Do! qu'il rit en dor-
rit.
Fls.
tr
(tr)
a tempo (meno mosso)
dreams!
-mant!
dreams!
-mant!
a tempo (meno mosso)
Fls.
rit.
pp

GOD REST YOU MERRY, GENTLEMEN

for Mixed Voices, S. A. T. B., Congregation, with Organ*

* Instrumentation: 2Fl, 2Ob, 2Cl, Bsn, 2Hn, 2Tpt, 2Tbn, B. Tbn, Tba, Timp, Perc, Strings. Woodwind, brass and percussion are optional if organ is available. Orchestral scores and parts are available on rental.

© Oxford University Press 1981. Photocopying this copyright material is ILLEGAL

Verses 2 and 4
Choir only (Congregation tacet)
Choir 1
mf 2. From God our heav'n-ly Fa - ther A bless-ed an-gel came, And
p 4. But when to Beth-le - hem they came Where-at this in-fant lay, They
Choir 2 and Organ
mf 2. Ah
p 4. Hum
(Verse 4: Organ tacet)
un - to cer-tain shep-herds Brought ti-dings of the same, How that in Beth-le-
found him in a man-ger Where ox-en feed on hay; His mo-ther Ma-ry
(with Congregation)
mf
-hem was born The Son of God by name: O — ti -dings of com - fort and
kneel-ing, Un - to the Lord did pray:
mf
O — ti -dings of com - fort and
mf
(Verse 4: with Organ)
After v. 2: D. C. for v. 3
After v. 4: straight on for v. 5
3
joy, com-fort and joy, O — ti - dings of com - fort and joy.
joy, — and joy, — O — ti - dings of com - fort and joy.
joy, and

Verse 5
Descant - Sopranos
f
5. Now to the Lord sing prai - ses, All you with - in this
All other voices
f
5. Now to the Lord sing prai - ses, All you with - in this
Gt. + Sw.
f
Tuba
Ped.
place, And with true love and bro - ther - hood Each
place, And with true love and bro - ther - hood Each
o - ther now em - brace; This ho - ly tide of
o - ther now em - brace; This ho - ly tide of

* originally: *All others doth deface*

Printed by Halstan

A SERVICE OF READINGS AND CAROLS

OPENING HYMN *O come, all ye faithful*

BIDDING PRAYER *(spoken by the Minister)*

Beloved in Christ, be it at this Christmas-tide our care and delight to hear again the message of the angels, and in heart and mind to go even unto Bethlehem and see this thing which is come to pass, and the Babe lying in a manger.

Therefore let us read and mark in Holy Scripture the tale of the loving purposes of God and the glorious redemption brought us by this Holy Child.

But first, let us pray for the needs of the whole world; for peace on earth and goodwill among all his people; for unity and brotherhood within the Church he came to build, and especially in this our congregation.

And because this would rejoice his heart, let us remember, in his name, the poor and helpless, the cold, the hungry, and the oppressed; the sick and them that mourn, the lonely and the unloved, the aged and the little children; all those who know not the Lord Jesus, or who love him not, or who by sin have grieved his heart of love.

Lastly, let us remember before God all those who rejoice with us, but upon another shore, and in a greater light, that multitude which no man can number, whose hope was in the Word made flesh, and with whom in this Lord Jesus we for evermore are one.

These prayers and praises let us humbly offer up to the throne of heaven, in the words which Christ himself hath taught us:

THE LORD'S PRAYER *(spoken by all)*

CAROLS *Lo, how a rose e'er blooming*
'Twas in the moon of winter time
Joy to the world!

HYMN *It came upon the midnight clear*

READING St Luke 2, vv. 1-7

CAROLS *Away in a manger*
Silent night

HYMN *O little town of Bethlehem*

READING St Luke 2, vv. 8-16

CAROLS *Rise up, shepherd, and follow*
In dulci jubilo
How great our joy!

HYMN *While shepherds watched their flocks*

READING St Matthew 2, vv. 1-11

CAROLS *Three kings of Orient*
Bring a torch, Jeannette, Isabella

READING Isaiah 60, vv. 1-6, 19 (*or* St John 1, vv. 1-14)

Minister The Lord be with you
Congregation And with thy spirit
Minister Let us pray

THE COLLECT FOR CHRISTMAS EVE *(spoken by the Minister)*

O God, who makes us glad with the yearly remembrance of the birth of thy only Son, Jesus Christ: Grant that as we joyfully receive him for our Redeemer, so we may with sure confidence behold him, when he shall come to be our judge; who liveth and reigneth with thee and the Holy Spirit, one God, world without end. *Amen.*

THE BLESSING *(spoken by the Minister)*

May he who by his Incarnation gathered into one things earthly and heavenly, fill you with the sweetness of inward peace and goodwill; and the blessing of God Almighty, the Father, the Son, and the Holy Spirit, be upon you and remain with you always. *Amen.*

CLOSING HYMN *God rest you merry, gentlemen*